Get the Bill

Teaching Tips

Red Level 2

This book focuses on the phoneme **/ll/**.

Before Reading

- Discuss the title. Ask readers what they think the book will be about.
- Sound out the words on page 3 together.

Read the Book

- Ask readers to use a finger to follow along with each word as it is read.
- Encourage readers to break down unfamiliar words into units of sound. Then, ask them to string the sounds together to create the words.
- Urge readers to point out when the focused phonics phoneme appears in the text.

After Reading

- Encourage children to reread the book independently or with a friend.
- Ask simple questions about the text to check for understanding. Have them find the pages that have the answers to your questions.

© 2024 Booklife Publishing
This edition is published by arrangement with Booklife Publishing.

North American adaptations © 2024 Jump!
5357 Penn Avenue South
Minneapolis, MN 55419
www.jumplibrary.com

Decodables by Jump! are published by Jump! Library.
All rights reserved. No part of this book may be reproduced in any form without written permission from the publisher.

Library of Congress Cataloging-in-Publication Data is available at www.loc.gov or upon request from the publisher.

ISBN: 979-8-88996-789-7 (hardcover)
ISBN: 979-8-88996-790-3 (paperback)
ISBN: 979-8-88996-791-0 (ebook)

Photo Credits
Images are courtesy of Shutterstock.com. With thanks to Getty Images, Thinkstock Photo and iStockphoto.
Cover – DNY59. 4–5 – Ebtikar, RusAKphoto. 6–7 – BarbaraGoreckaPhotography, Peter Hermes Furian, David Tadevosian.
8–9 – Phil Date, Zurijeta. 10–11 – Andrey_Popov, Pressmaster. 14–15 – Shutterstock.

Can you find these words in the book?

bell

bill

dill

doll

I can sit. The doll can sit.

I can tell him to fill it.

It has dill on it.

The bell is hit.

Bell

It is not dull. It is good!

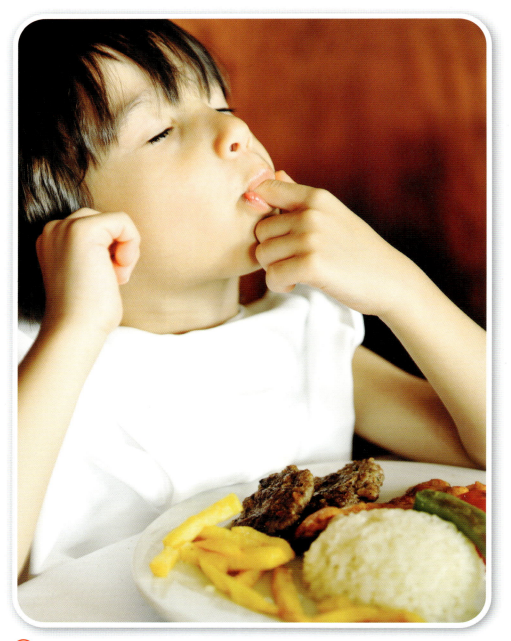

The man can sell it to us.

It is the bill.

Mom pays the bill. Let us go!

Can you say this sound and draw it with your finger?

Can you say this word and draw it with your finger?

What other words do you know that have the letters /ll/?

shell

football

hill

Practice reading the book again:

I can sit. The doll can sit.
I can tell him to fill it.
It has dill on it.
The bell is hit.
It is not dull. It is good!
The man can sell it to us.
It is the bill.
Mom pays the bill. Let us go!